Following the Rules

Katie Peters

GRL Consultants,
Diane Craig and Monica Marx,
Certified Literacy Specialists

Pull Ahead Readers
People Smarts

Lerner Publications ◆ Minneapolis

Note from a GRL Consultant
This Pull Ahead leveled book has been carefully designed for beginning readers. A team of guided reading literacy experts has reviewed and leveled the book to ensure readers pull ahead and experience success.

Lerner Publications Company
An imprint of Lerner Publishing Group, Inc.
241 First Avenue North
Minneapolis, MN 55401 USA

For reading levels and more information, look up this title at www.lernerbooks.com.

Main body text set in Memphis Pro 24/39
Typeface provided by Linotype

Photo Acknowledgments
The images in this book are used with the permission of: © Ariel Skelley/Getty Images, pp. 14–15; © FatCamera/Getty Images, pp. 8–9, 10–11; © Jupiterimages/Getty Images, pp. 12–13, 16 (center); © Noel Hendrickson/Getty Images, pp. 6–7, 16 (left); © ronniechua/Getty Images, p. 3; © SDI Productions/Getty Images, pp. 4–5, 16 (right).

Front cover: © Jose Luis Pelaez Inc/Getty Images.

Library of Congress Cataloging-in-Publication Data

Names: Peters, Katie, author.
Title: Following the rules / Katie Peters.
Description: Minneapolis : Lerner Publications 2022. | Series: Be a good sport. Pull ahead readers. People smarts. Nonfiction | Includes index. | Audience: Ages 4–7 | Audience: Grades K–1 | Summary: "From baseball to tag to cards, every game has rules to follow. Learn how to be a good sport by playing by the rules. Pairs with the fiction title Not Yet!"— Provided by publisher.
Identifiers: LCCN 2021010300 (print) | LCCN 2021010301 (ebook) | ISBN 9781728440941 (library binding) | ISBN 9781728444437 (ebook)
Subjects: LCSH: Sports—Rules—Juvenile literature. | Games—Rules—Juenile liteature. | Sportsmanship—Juvenile literature.
Classification: LCC GV731 .P47 2022 (print) | LCC GV731 (ebook) | DDC 796—dc23

LC record available at https://lccn.loc.gov/2021010300
LC ebook record available at https://lccn.loc.gov/2021010301

Manufactured in the United States of America
1 – CG – 12/15/21

Table of Contents

Following the Rules

I like to play soccer. My coach teaches me the rules. I kick the ball with my feet.

I like to play basketball. My mom teaches me the rules. I dribble the ball.

I like to play baseball. My dad teaches me the rules. If I get three strikes, I am out.

I like to play tag. My friend teaches me the rules. If I get tagged, I am it.

I like to play cards. My grandma teaches me the rules. We play many card games.

Woodlake

Games have rules.
Following the rules
makes playing fun.

Can you think of a time when you followed the rules?

Did You See It?

basketball

cards

soccer ball

Index